Al

Adane Nega Tarekegn

A Quick Guide To An Introduction to Expert System Using PROLOG

Alemu Kumilachew Tegegnie
Adane Nega Tarekegn

A Quick Guide To An Introduction to Expert System Using PROLOG

LAP LAMBERT Academic Publishing

Impressum / Imprint
Bibliografische Information der Deutschen Nationalbibliothek: Die Deutsche Nationalbibliothek verzeichnet diese Publikation in der Deutschen Nationalbibliografie; detaillierte bibliografische Daten sind im Internet über http://dnb.d-nb.de abrufbar.
Alle in diesem Buch genannten Marken und Produktnamen unterliegen warenzeichen-, marken- oder patentrechtlichem Schutz bzw. sind Warenzeichen oder eingetragene Warenzeichen der jeweiligen Inhaber. Die Wiedergabe von Marken, Produktnamen, Gebrauchsnamen, Handelsnamen, Warenbezeichnungen u.s.w. in diesem Werk berechtigt auch ohne besondere Kennzeichnung nicht zu der Annahme, dass solche Namen im Sinne der Warenzeichen- und Markenschutzgesetzgebung als frei zu betrachten wären und daher von jedermann benutzt werden dürften.

Bibliographic information published by the Deutsche Nationalbibliothek: The Deutsche Nationalbibliothek lists this publication in the Deutsche Nationalbibliografie; detailed bibliographic data are available in the Internet at http://dnb.d-nb.de.
Any brand names and product names mentioned in this book are subject to trademark, brand or patent protection and are trademarks or registered trademarks of their respective holders. The use of brand names, product names, common names, trade names, product descriptions etc. even without a particular marking in this work is in no way to be construed to mean that such names may be regarded as unrestricted in respect of trademark and brand protection legislation and could thus be used by anyone.

Coverbild / Cover image: www.ingimage.com

Verlag / Publisher:
LAP LAMBERT Academic Publishing
ist ein Imprint der / is a trademark of
OmniScriptum GmbH & Co. KG
Heinrich-Böcking-Str. 6-8, 66121 Saarbrücken, Deutschland / Germany
Email: info@lap-publishing.com

Herstellung: siehe letzte Seite /
Printed at: see last page
ISBN: 978-3-659-74915-5

Acknowledgement

First and foremost, we would like to thank our colleague Workineh Chekol for standing beside us throughout our career and writing this book. He has been our inspiration and motivation for continuing to improve our knowledge and move our career forward. Second, we appreciate Biruk Adane for his valuable input, comments and editing to write a book.

Throughout the process of writing this book, many individuals from Bahirdar University have taken time out to help us out. We would like to say thank you to all of them.

Table of Contents

Abbreviations

AI	Artificial Intelligence
ES	Expert System
KBS	Knowledge Based systems
PROLOG	PROgramming in LOGic
SQL	Structured Query Languages
HTML	Hyper Text Markup Languages

Chapter One

Introduction to Expert Systems

At the end of this session, learners should be able to:

- Define Artificial Intelligence, Expert system and understand their difference.

- Understand characteristics of AI systems and their difference among database systems.

- Understand the major components of experts system.

- Understand how expert systems work.

- Identify the application of expert systems.

- Understand the reasoning strategies of expert systems.

Overview of Artificial intelligence

Expert System is one of the specific fields of Artificial Intelligence (AI). The field of artificial intelligence (AI) is concerned with methods of developing systems that display aspects of intelligent behavior. These systems are designed to imitate the human capabilities of thinking and sensing. AI systems are characterized by the use symbols for processing and its non-algorithmic nature.

Symbolic Processing - In AI applications, computers process symbols rather than numbers or letters. AI applications process strings of characters that represent real-

1

world entities or concepts. Symbols can be arranged in structures such as lists, hierarchies, or networks. These structures show how symbols relate to each other.

Non-algorithmic Processing - Computer programs outside the AI domain are programmed algorithms; that is, fully specified step-by-step procedures that define a solution to the problem. The actions of a knowledge-based AI system depend to a far greater degree on the situation where it is used.

Expert Systems

The most important applied area of AI is the field of expert systems. An *expert system* (ES) is a knowledge-based system that employs knowledge about its application domain and uses an inferencing (reason) procedure to solve problems that would otherwise require human competence or expertise. The power of expert systems stems primarily from the specific knowledge about a narrow domain stored in the expert system's *knowledge base*.

It is important to stress to students that expert systems are assistants to decision makers and not substitutes for them. Expert systems do not have human capabilities. They use a knowledge base of a particular domain and bring that knowledge to bear on the facts of the particular situation at hand. The knowledge base of an ES also contains *heuristic knowledge -* rules of thumb used by human experts who work in the domain.

In short,

> **Expert System = Expert + System**
>
> **Expert** = *somebody with a great deal of knowledge about, or skill, training, or experience in, a particular field or activity e.g. a medical expert*
>
> **System** = *a set of interrelated objects/components working together to achieve a common objective*
>
> **Expert system** = *a set of logical and technical components designed to simulate the reasoning of a human expert, who has great deal of knowledge, skill, training, or experience in a certain subject area [based on symbolic processing].*

The Applications of Expert Systems

The spectrum of applications of expert systems technology to industrial and commercial problems is so wide as to defy easy characterization. The applications find their way into most areas of knowledge work. They are as varied as helping salespersons sell modular factory-built homes to helping NASA plan the maintenance of a space shuttle in preparation for its next flight. Applications tend to cluster into seven major classes.

Diagnosis and Troubleshooting of Devices and Systems of All Kinds - this class comprises systems that deduce faults and suggest corrective actions for a malfunctioning device or process. Medical diagnosis was one of the first knowledge areas to which ES technology was applied, but diagnosis of engineered

3

systems quickly surpassed medical diagnosis. There are probably more diagnostic applications of ES than any other type. The diagnostic problem can be stated in the abstract as: given the evidence presenting itself, what is the underlying problem/reason/cause?

Planning and Scheduling - systems that fall into this class analyze a set of one or more potentially complex and interacting goals in order to determine a set of actions to achieve those goals, and/or provide a detailed temporal ordering of those actions, taking into account personnel, materiel, and other constraints. This class has great commercial potential, which has been recognized. Examples involve airline scheduling of flights, personnel, and gates; manufacturing job-shop scheduling; and manufacturing process planning.

Configuration of Manufactured Objects from Subassemblies - configuration, whereby a solution to a problem is synthesized from a given set of elements related by a set of constraints, is historically one of the most important of expert system applications. Configuration applications were pioneered by computer companies as a means of facilitating the manufacture of semi-custom minicomputers. The technique has found its way into use in many different industries, for example, modular home building, manufacturing, and other problems involving complex engineering design and manufacturing.

4

Financial Decision Making - the financial services industry has been a vigorous user of expert system techniques. Advisory programs have been created to assist bankers in determining whether to make loans to businesses and individuals. Insurance companies have used expert systems to assess the risk presented by the customer and to determine a price for the insurance. A typical application in the financial markets is in foreign exchange trading.

Knowledge Publishing - this is a relatively new, but also potentially explosive area. The primary function of the expert system is to deliver knowledge that is relevant to the user's problem, in the context of the user's problem. The two most widely distributed expert systems in the world are in this category. The first is an advisor which counsels a user on appropriate grammatical usage in a text. The second is a tax advisor that accompanies a tax preparation program and advises the user on tax strategy, tactics, and individual tax policy.

Process Monitoring and Control - systems falling in this class analyze real-time data from physical devices with the goal of noticing anomalies, predicting trends, and controlling for both optimality and failure correction. Examples of real-time systems that actively monitor processes can be found in the steel making and oil refining industries.

Design and Manufacturing - these systems assist in the design of physical devices and processes, ranging from high-level conceptual design of abstract entities all the way to factory floor configuration of manufacturing processes.

How Expert Systems Work

The strength of an ES derives from its *knowledge base* - an organized collection of facts and heuristics about the system's domain. An ES is built in a process known as *knowledge engineering*, during which knowledge about the domain is acquired from human experts and other sources by knowledge engineers. The accumulation of knowledge in knowledge bases, from which conclusions are to be drawn by the *inference engine*, is the hallmark of an expert system.

Characteristics of Expert system

Expert systems are characterized by:

- ✓ Domain specificity: ES operates in a micro-world where particular kind of problem solving is required.
- ✓ Special Programming Languages: declarative languages such as LISP and Prolog
    - Efficient mix of integer and real variables
    - Good memory-management procedures

- Extensive data-manipulation routines
- Incremental compilation
- Tagged memory architecture
- Optimization of the systems environment
- Efficient search procedures

✓ ES reasons over representation of human knowledge.

✓ ES solves problems of genuine scientific or commercial interest through application of heuristic or approximate methods.

✓ ES, unlike 'algorithmic' methods, are not guaranteed to succeed.

✓ ES presents solutions in a reasonable time.

✓ ES provide correct solutions most of the time-equal to or better than accuracy rate expected from a human expert.

✓ Es follow difficult programs as good as or better than human experts.

✓ ES posse's vast quantities of domain specific knowledge to the minute details.

✓ ES communicates with users in its own natural language.

✓ ES provides extensive facilities for symbolic process rather than numeric process

The needs of Expert system

Expert systems are necessitated by the limitations associated with conventional human decision-making processes, including:

- ✓ Human expertise is very scarce.
- ✓ Humans get tired from physical or mental workload.
- ✓ Humans forget crucial details of a problem.
- ✓ Humans are inconsistent in their day-to-day decisions.
- ✓ Humans have limited working memory.
- ✓ Humans are unable to comprehend large amounts of data quickly.
- ✓ Humans are unable to retain large amounts of data in memory.
- ✓ Humans are slow in recalling information stored in memory.
- ✓ Humans are subject to deliberate or inadvertent bias in their actions.
- ✓ Humans can deliberately avoid decision responsibilities.
- ✓ Humans lie, hide, and die.

Components of Expert Systems

Any typical Expert system involves six basic components: User interface, Search engine, Knowledge base, memory and explanation and knowledge editor components. The following figure describes the basic components of expert system.

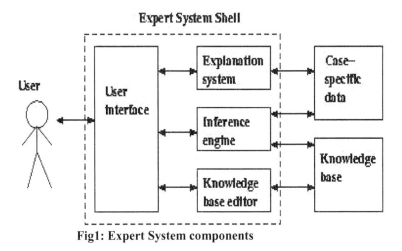

Fig1: Expert System components

Knowledge representation & Knowledge Base

The knowledge base of an ES contains both factual and heuristic knowledge. *Knowledge representation* is the method used to organize the knowledge in the knowledge base. Knowledge bases must represent notions as actions to be taken under circumstances, causality, time, dependencies, goals, and other higher-level concepts. Several methods of knowledge representation can be drawn upon. Two of these methods include:

Frame-based systems - these are employed for building very powerful ESs. A frame specifies the attributes of a complex object and frames for various object types which have specified relationships. In frame based systems, the values of a

9

unique object attribute is defined and put in a frame/slot where common values are filled in higher level classes.

Production rules - rules are the most common method of knowledge representation used in business. *Rule-based expert systems* are expert systems in which the knowledge is represented by production rules. The ***explanation facility*** explains how the system arrived at the recommendation. Depending on the tool used to implement the expert system, the explanation may be either in a natural language or simply a listing of rule numbers.

Inference Engine

The inference engine allows the expert system drive a solution for a specific problem. It

1. Combines the facts of a specific case with the knowledge contained in the knowledge base to come up with a recommendation. In a rule-based expert system, the inference engine controls the order in which production rules are applied and resolves conflicts if more than one rule is applicable at a given time.

2. Directs the user interface to query the user for any information it needs for further inferencing.

The facts of the given case are entered into the *working memory*, which acts as a blackboard, accumulating the knowledge about the case at hand. The inference engine repeatedly applies the rules to the working memory, adding new information (obtained from the rules conclusions) to it, until a goal state is produced or confirmed. Inference engines for rule-based systems generally work by either forward or backward chaining of rules. Two strategies are:

Forward chaining - is a data-driven strategy. The inference process moves from the facts of the case to a goal (conclusion). The strategy is thus driven by the facts available in the working memory and by the premises that can be satisfied. The inference engine attempts to match the condition (IF) part of each rule in the knowledge base with the facts currently available in the working memory. If several rules match, a conflict resolution procedure is invoked; for example, the lowest-numbered rule that adds new information to the working memory is fired. The conclusion of the firing rule is added to the working memory.

Forward-chaining systems are commonly used to solve more open-ended problems of a design or planning nature, such as, for example, establishing the configuration of a complex product.

Backward chaining - the inference engine attempts to match the assumed (hypothesized) conclusion - the goal or subgoal state - with the conclusion (THEN) part of the rule. If such a rule is found, its premise becomes the new subgoal. In an ES with few possible goal states, this is a good strategy to pursue. If a hypothesized goal state cannot be supported by the premises, the system will attempt to prove another goal state. Thus, possible conclusions are review until a goal state that can be supported by the premises is encountered.

Backward chaining is best suited for applications in which the possible conclusions are limited in number and well defined. Classification or diagnosis type systems, in which each of several possible conclusions can be checked to see if it is supported by the data, are typical applications.

In short,

Forward reasoning - Facts are given. What is the conclusion?

    A set of known facts is given (in WM); apply rules to derive new facts as conclusions (forward chaining of rules) until you come up with a requested final goal fact.

Backward reasoning - Hypothesis (goal) is given. Is it supported by facts?

    A hypothesis (goal fact) is given; try to derive it based on a set of given initial facts using sub-goals (backward chaining of rules) until goal is grounded in initial facts

---

The following chart illustrates the use of forward and backward chaining strategies in determining a grade.

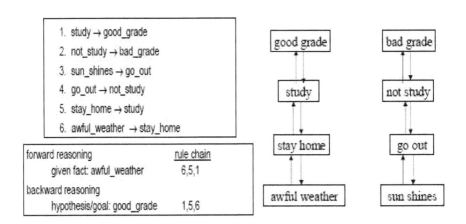

Fig2. Forward reasoning and backward reasoning

Uncertainty and Fuzzy Logic

Fuzzy logic is a method of reasoning that resembles human reasoning since it allows for approximate values and inferences and incomplete or ambiguous data (fuzzy data). Fuzzy logic is a method of choice for handling uncertainty in some expert systems. Expert systems with fuzzy-logic capabilities thus allow for more flexible and creative handling of problems. These systems are used, for example, to control manufacturing processes. They are handled using statistical methods and symbolic processing techniques.

Roles in Expert System Development

Expert system development requires a series of developmental steps and involves stakeholders having significant roles in each step. Expert system development process involves the expert, knowledge engineer and user which play fundamental roles in building expert systems.

1. *Expert* - Successful ES systems depend on the experience and application of knowledge that the people can bring to it during its development. Large systems generally require multiple experts.

2. *Knowledge engineer* - The knowledge engineer has a dual task. This person should be able to elicit knowledge from the expert, gradually gaining an understanding of an area of expertise. Intelligence, tact, empathy, and proficiency in specific techniques of knowledge acquisition are all required of a knowledge engineer.

Knowledge-acquisition techniques include conducting interviews with varying degrees of structure, protocol analysis, observation of experts at work, and analysis of cases. On the other hand, the knowledge engineer must also select a tool appropriate for the project and use it to represent the knowledge with the application of the *knowledge acquisition facility*.

3. *User* - A system developed by an end user with a simple shell, is built rather quickly an inexpensively. Larger systems are built in an organized development effort. A prototype-oriented iterative development strategy is commonly used. ESs lends them particularly well to prototyping.

Development and Maintenance of Expert Systems

Steps in the methodology for the iterative process of ES development and maintenance include:

1. Problem Identification and Feasibility Analysis:
   - The problem must be suitable for an expert system to solve it.
   - must find an expert for the project
   - cost-effectiveness of the system has to be established (feasibility)

2. System Design and ES Technology Identification:
   - The system is being designed. The needed degree of integration with other subsystems and databases is established concepts that best represent the domain knowledge are worked out
   - the best way to represent the knowledge and to perform inference should be established with sample cases.

3. Development of Prototype:
   - Knowledge engineer works with the expert to place the initial kernel of knowledge in the knowledge base.
   - knowledge needs to be expressed in the language of the specific tool chosen for the project

4. Testing and Refinement of Prototype:
   - Using sample cases, the prototype is tested, and deficiencies in performance are noted. End users test the prototypes of the ES.

5. Complete and Field the ES:
   - The interaction of the ES with all elements of its environment, including users and other information systems, is ensured and tested.
   - ES is documented and user training is conducted

6. Maintain the System:
   - The system is kept current primarily by updating its knowledge base.
   - Interfaces with other information systems have to be maintained as well, as those systems evolve.

Review questions

1. Define Artificial Intelligence (AI)? What characterizes AI Systems and how are they different from database systems?

2. Define Expert systems and compare and contrast the characteristics of AI and Expert systems.

3. Describe the components of expert systems and discuss their role.

4. Explain the difference between forward and back ward reasoning strategy in expert systems processing.

5. Discuss the difference between expert systems and other information systems.

6. Explain the stakeholders of expert system development , their roles, and development steps

Chapter Two

Expert System Languages

At the end of this session, learners should be able to:

- Identify expert system languages
- Understand the difference between declarative and procedural languages.
- Understand PROLOG as a programming language with its own syntax and semantics
- Differentiate PROLOG with other programming languages
- Understand the operating environments of PROLOG
- understand the reasons by which declarative languages are used as programming language for knowledge (expert) based systems
- understand special features of declarative languages (such as PROLOG) for "data" representation
- Understand the description of the real world phenomenon

Declarative vs Procedural Knowledge

Declarative knowledge involves knowing that something is the case - that J is the tenth letter of the alphabet, that Paris is the capital of France. Declarative knowledge is conscious; it can often be verbalized. Met linguistic knowledge, or knowledge about a linguistic form, is declarative knowledge.

Procedural knowledge involves knowing how to do something - ride a bike, for example. We may not be able to explain how we do it. Procedural knowledge involves implicit learning, which a learner may not be aware of, and may involve being able to use a particular form to understand or produce language without necessarily being able to explain it.

More distinctions:

- ✓ Procedural knowledge, in a nutshell, knows how to do something. It contrasts with declarative knowledge, which is knowledge about something

- ✓ Declarative knowledge enables a student to describe a rule and perhaps apply it in a drill or a gap-fill. Procedural knowledge, on the other hand, enables the student to apply that rule in real language use.

- ✓ Procedural programming requires that the programmer tell the computer what to do. That is, *how* to get the output for the range of required inputs. The programmer must know an appropriate algorithm.

- ✓ Declarative programming requires a more descriptive style. The programmer must know *what* relationships hold between various entities. *Pure* Prolog allows a program to be read either declaratively or procedurally. This dual semantics is attractive.

✓ Procedural programming is sometimes used as a synonym for imperative programming (specifying the steps the program must take to reach the desired state), but can also refer (as in this article) to a programming paradigm based upon the concept of the procedure call. Procedures, also known as routines, subroutines, methods, or functions (not to be confused with mathematical functions, but similar to those used in functional programming) simply contain a series of computational steps to be carried out. Any given procedure might be called at any point during a program's execution, including by other procedures or itself.

✓ Procedural programming is often a better choice than simple sequential or unstructured programming in many situations which involve moderate complexity or which require significant ease of maintainability.

✓ Possible benefits:

> The ability to re-use the same code at different places in the program without copying it.

> An easier way to keep track of program flow than a collection of "GOTO" or "JUMP" statement (which can turn a large, complicated program into so-called "spaghetti code").

> The ability to be strongly modular or structured.

- ✓ In procedural programming, the program is written as a collection of actions (a procedure) that are carried out in sequence, one after the other. The order is important. A procedure is sometimes termed an algorithm.

- ✓ An ingredient of procedural programming is the idea of state. The actions in a program change the value of data items, usually termed variables. As the program executes, the values of variables change. At any point in time the variables have a set of values, which is their state.

- ✓ Declarative programming is a term with two distinct meanings, both of which are in current use.

  According to one definition, a program is "declarative" if it describes what something is like, rather than how to create it. For example, HTML web pages are declarative because they describe what the page should contain — title, text, images — but not how to actually display the page on a computer screen. This is a different approach from imperative programming languages such as Fortran, C, and Java, which require the programmer to specify an algorithm to be run.

- ✓ According to a different definition, a program is "declarative" if it is written in a purely functional programming language, logic programming language, or constraint programming language. The phrase "declarative language" is sometimes used to describe all such programming languages as a group, and to contrast them against imperative languages.

✓ Similarly, it is possible to write programs in a declarative style even in an imperative programming language. This is usually done by encapsulating non-declarative details inside a library or framework.

✓ In a declarative program you write (declare) a data structure that is processed by a standard algorithm (for that language) to produce the desired result. A declarative language, like all languages, has a syntax describing how the words in the language may be combined, and a semantics describing how sentences in the language correspond to a program's output.

PROLOG as an Expert System Language

What is a PROLOG Program?

Prolog is invented early seventies by Alain Colmerauer in France and Robert Kowalski in Britain. Prolog is Programmation en Logique (Programming in Logic). Prolog is a declarative programming language unlike most common programming languages such as C++, JAVA, PASCAL, etc. In a declarative language, the programmer specifies a goal to be achieved and the Prolog system works out how to achieve it. In the other hand, most traditional programming languages are said to be **procedural, where a** procedural programmer must specify in detail how to solve a problem like the statements below:

- mix ingredients;

- beat until smooth;

- bake for 20 minutes in a moderate oven;

- remove tin from oven;

- put on bench;

- close oven;

- turn off oven;

Whereas in a purely declarative languages, the programmer only states what the problem is and leaves the rest to the language system. We'll see specific, simple examples of cases where Prolog fits really well shortly

Prolog can be separated in two parts:

The Program

The program, sometimes called Database is a text file (*.pl) that contain the facts and rules that will be used by the user of the program. It contains all the relations that make this program.

The Query

When you launch a program you are in query mode. This mode is represented by the sign ? - at the beginning of the line. In query mode you ask questions about relations described in the program.

Getting started with Prolog

To get started with prolog; you need to know how to:-

- Launch the development environment (there are different development environments for prolog but we will use SWI-Prolog here)
- Start->all programs->SWI-Prolog->Prolog
- Edit the source code
- Though we do have different options we will use notepad first, You have to save your source file with *.pl* extension.
- Load the source file for querying , and
- Click on the file menu in the SWI-Prolog window->choose Consult -> Load file into prolog dialog box will appear->then browse and locate your file-> finally click open.
- Double clicking the prolog file (file.pl) from its location can also used to open in query mode.
- Query the knowledgebase

Unlike imperative (procedural) programming languages we didn't run a standalone exe file generated as a result of compilation for execution. Rather we query (ask) the loaded program and the program logically responds for us. So to query simply type your queries following the prolog system prompt (? -) .

Applications of Prolog

PROLOG can be applied in areas where knowledge is the one you acquire, represent and manipulate as a central processing unit. Moreover, your problem requires some kind of intelligence that follows from a represented knowledge. In addition to expert systems, some applications of Prolog include:

- intelligent data base retrieval
- natural language understanding
- specification language
- machine learning
- robot planning
- automated reasoning
- problem solving

Facts and Rules in PROLOG

Programming in Prolog

You can program your task using prolog in three ways. First, declare **facts** describing explicit relationships between objects and properties objects might have (e.g. Mary likes pizza, grass has_colour green, Fido is_a_dog, Mizuki taught Paul Japanese). Declaration of facts involves a special editor.

Second, define **rules** defining implicit relationships between objects (e.g. the sister rule above) and/or rules defining implicit object properties (e.g. X is a parent if there is a Y such that Y is a child of X).

Lastly, one then uses the system by asking questions above relationships between objects, and/or about object properties (e.g. does Mary like pizza? is Joe a parent?) The declaration of clauses - which *either facts or rules describing the real world phenomenon* –requires a special editor. Common editor software includes Note pad, Note Pad++ or any other editors can be used.

Facts

Facts describe the relation between different objects and are independent of each other. They are the properties of objects, or relationships between objects. For example,

"Dr Turing lectures in course 9020" is a fact, which is written in Prolog as:

lectures(turing, 9020).

You have to note that in PROLOG:

- Names of properties/relationships begin with lower case letters.

- the relationship name appears as the first term

- Objects appear as comma-separated arguments within parentheses.

- A period "." must end a fact.

- Objects also begin with lower case letters. They also can begin with digits (like 9020), and can be strings of characters enclosed in quotes (as in reads (fred, "War and Peace")).

- Lectures (turing, 9020). is also called a *predicate* – a function that performs some kind of action which always have the aforementioned form.

Note:- facts describe the world as a it is "fact". The represented statement is always refers it is true.

Syntax: - Predicate (atom or compound term) followed by a full stop.

Facts with arguments

More complicated facts consist of a relation and the items that this refers to. These items are called arguments. Facts can have arbitrary number of arguments from zero upwards. A general model is shown below:

Relation (<argument1>,<argument2>,....,<argumentN>).

The arguments can be any legal Prolog term. The basic Prolog terms are an integer, an atom, a variable or a structure. Various Prolog implementations enhance this basic list with other data types, such as floating point numbers, or strings.

Example: likes(john,mary).

> The followings are legal atoms:
  hello
  zz42
  two_words

> The followings are not legal atoms:
  Hello

  4hello

  _Hello

  two words

  two-words

You can use single quotes to make any character combination a legal atom.

'two words'

'UpperCase'

'12444'

'etc...'

The fact likes(john,mary), say that there is a relation between john and mary. It can be read as either john likes mary or mary likes john. This reversibility can be very useful to the programmer; however it can also be a source of mistakes. You have to be clear on how you intend to interpret the relation.

The number of arguments is the **arity** of the predicate. A predicate with two arguments will be called by predicate_name/2. You can have different predicates with the same name if they have a different arity.

Relations

Prolog programs specify *relationships* among objects and properties of objects. When we say, "John owns the book", we are declaring the ownership relationship between two objects: John and the book. When we ask, "Does John own the book?" we are trying to find out about a relationship.

Relationships can also be rules such as:

Two people are sisters **if**

they are both female **and**

they have the same parents.

A rule allows us to find out about a relationship even if the relationship isn't explicitly stated as a fact. As usual in programming, you need to be a bit careful how you phrase things. The following would be better:

A and B are sisters **if**
A and B are both female **and**
they have the same father **and**
they have the same mother **and**
A is not the same as B

For example facts about a hypothetical computer science department:

% lectures(X, Y): person X lectures in course Y	*% studies(X, Y): person X studies in course Y*	*%year(X, Y): person X is in year Y*
lectures(turing, 9020).	studies(fred, 9020).	year(fred, 1).
lectures(codd, 9311).	studies(jack, 9311).	year(jack, 2).
lectures(backus, 9021).	studies(jill, 9314).	year(jill, 2).
lectures(ritchie, 9201).	studies(jill, 9414).	year(henry, 4).
lectures(minsky, 9414).	studies(henry, 9414).	
lectures(codd, 9314).	studies(henry, 9314).	

Note that, together, these facts form Prolog's *database (often called knowledgebase)*

How to Query

Once we have a database of facts (and, soon, rules) we can ask questions about the stored information.

Example:

```
eats(fred,oranges).    /* 'Fred eats oranges' */
eats(tony,apple).      /* 'Tony eats apple'   */
eats(john,apple).      /* 'John eats apple'   */
```

If we now ask some queries we would get the following things:

?- eats(fred,oranges).

/* does this match anything in the knowledge base? */

yes

/* yes, that matchs the first clause */

?- eats(john,apple).

yes

?- eats(mike,apple).

no

/* there is no relation between mike and apple */

Based on the facts we represented earlier, we can ask the prolog system prompt by typing a query. Prolog answers our query by referring the knowledge base. You have to note that:

- In SWI Prolog, queries are terminated by a full stop.

- To answer this query, Prolog consults its database to see if this is a known fact.

- Prolog replies Yes/No or True/False according the existence facts and relations in the knowledge base.

Another example query

?- *lectures(codd, 9020).*

false.

- if answer is true., the query *succeeded*

- if answer is false., the query *failed.*

Many early versions of Prolog, including early versions of SWI-Prolog, say No instead of false. In the latest version of SWI Prolog, it no longer says "No." but says "false." instead. The use of lower case for code is critical. Prolog is not being intelligent about this - it would not see a difference between this query and

     lectures(fred, 9020). or lectures(xyzzy, 9020).

Though a person inspecting the database can see that fred is a student, not a lecturer, and that xyzzy is neither student nor lecturer.

Variables and Unification

Variables

Suppose we want to ask, "What course does Turing teach"? This could be written as:

     Is there a course, X, that Turing teaches?

The variable X stands for an object that the questioner does not know about yet.

    X   /* a single capital letter   */

    VaRiAbLe   /* a word beginning with an upper case letter */

    Two_words /* two words separated with an underscore */

To answer the question, Prolog has to find out the value of X, if it exists. As long as we do not know the value of a variable it is said to be *unbound*. Whereas, when a value is found, the variable is said to *bound* to that value. The name of a variable must begin with a capital letter or an underscore character, "_".

- To ask Prolog to find the course that Turing teaches, enter this:

    ?- lectures(turing, Course).

    Course = 9020   output from Prolog

- To ask which course(s) Prof. Codd teaches, we may ask,

    ?- lectures(codd , Course).

    Course = 9311 ;   type ";" to get next solution

    Course = 9314

    ?-

If Prolog can tell that there are no more solutions, it just gives you the ?- prompt for a new query, as here. If Prolog can't tell, it will let you type ; again, and then if there is no further solution, report false/no.

    ?- eats(fred,What).

    What=apple ;

    What=oranges ;

    false

Prolog can find all possible ways to answer a query, unless you explicitly tell it not to do using codes (see *cut*, later).

Variables unification

Consider this example of program that could be used by a library:

book(1,title1,author1).

book(2,title2,author1).

book(3,title3,author2).

book(4,title4,author3).

Now if we want to know if we have a book from the author2 we can ask:

?- book(_,_,author2).

yes

If we want to know which book from the author1 we have:

?- book(_,X,author1).

X=title1 ;

X=title2 ;

Conjunctions of Goals in Queries

How do we ask, "Does Turing teach Fred"? This means finding out if Turing lectures in a course that Fred studies.

?- *lectures(turing, Course), studies(fred, Course).*

i.e. "Turing lectures in course, Course **and** Fred studies (the same) Course".

The question consists of two *goals*. To answer this question, Prolog must find a single value for *Course*, that satisfies both goals. Read the comma, ",", as **and**.

However, note that Prolog will evaluate the two goals left-to-right. In pure logic, P1 ∧ P2 is the same as P2 ∧ P1. In Prolog, there is the practical consideration of which goal should be evaluated first - the code might be more efficient one way or the other. In particular, in "P1, P2", if P1 fails, then P2 does not need to be evaluated at all. This is sometimes referred to as a "conditional-and".

Disjunctions of Goals in Queries

What about **or** (i.e. disjunction)? It turns out explicit **or**s aren't needed much in Prolog. There is a way to write **or**: (";"). The reason **or**s aren't needed much is that

> head :- body1.
>
> head :- body2.
>
> has the same effect as
>
> head :- body1 ; body2.

Avoid using ; if you can, at least until you have learned how to manage without it. While some uses of ; are harmless, others can make your code hard to follow.

Backtracking in Prolog

Who does Codd teach?

> *?- lectures(codd, Course), studies(Student, Course).*
> Course = 9311
> Student = jack ;
> Course = 9314

Student = jill ;

Course = 9314

Student = henry ;

Prolog solves this problem by proceeding left to right and then *backtracking*. When given the initial query, Prolog starts by trying to solve

lectures(codd, Course).

There are six lectures clauses, but only two have codd as their first argument. Prolog uses the first clause that refers to codd: *lectures(codd, 9311).* With Course = 9311, it tries to satisfy the next goal, *studies(Student, 9311).* It finds the fact *studies(jack, 9311).* and hence the first solution: (Course = 9311, Student = jack). After the first solution is found, Prolog retraces its steps up the tree and looks for alternative solutions.

- First it looks for other students studying 9311 (but finds none).

- Then it

  - backs up

  - rebinds Course to 9314,

  - goes down the lectures(codd, 9314) branch

  - tries studies(Student, 9314),

  - finds the other two solutions:

    (Course = 9314, Student = jill)

    and (Course = 9314, Student = henry).

To picture what happens when Prolog tries to find a solution and backtracks, we draw a "proof tree":

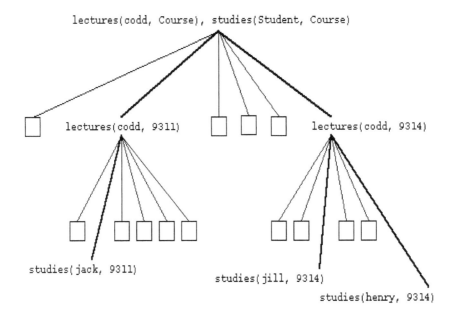

Rules

So far we have looked at how to represent facts and to query them. Now we move on to rules. Rules allow us to make conditional statements about our world. Each rule can have several variations, called clauses. These clauses give us different choices about how to perform inference about our world.

In prolog rules are used in the process of decision making and can deduce new facts from existing ones. Rules are of the form *Head:- Body.* In order for the head to be true all the statements in the body must be true. Like facts, they have to be followed by a full stop.

Example: The previous question can be restated as a general rule:

> One person, Teacher, teaches another person, Student *if*
>
> > Teacher lectures in a course, Course *and*
> >
> > Student studies Course.

In Prolog this is written as:

> teaches(Teacher, Student) :-
>
> > lectures(Teacher, Course),
> >
> > studies(Student, Course).

What Prolog will reply to this query?

> ?- teaches(codd, Student).

Note that, facts are *unit clauses* and rules are *non-unit clauses*.

Syntax

- ":-" means "if" or "is implied by". Also called the *neck* symbol.

- The left hand side of the neck is called the *head*.

- The right hand side of the neck is called the *body*.

- The comma, ",", separating the goals, stands for *and*.

Tracing Execution

more_advanced(S1, S2) :-

    year(S1, Year1),

    year(S2, Year2),

    Year1 > Year2.

?- *trace.*	
true.	
[trace] ?- *more_advanced(henry, fred).*	bind S1 to henry, S2 to fred
Call: more_advanced(henry, fred) ? *	test 1st goal in body of rule
Call: year(henry, _L205) ?	succeeds, binds Year1 to 4
Exit: year(henry, 4) ?	test 2nd goal in body of rule
Call: year(fred, _L206) ?	succeeds, binds Year2 to 1
Exit: year(fred, 1) ?	test 3rd goal: Year1 > Year2
^ Call: 4>1 ?	succeeds
^ Exit: 4>1 ?	succeeds
Exit: more_advanced(henry, fred) ?	
true.	
[debug] ?- *notrace.*	

* The ? is a prompt. Press the return key at end of each line of tracing. Prolog will echo the <return> as creep, and then print the next line of tracing. The "creep"s have been removed in the table above, to reduce clutter.

true., false., or true

Sometimes, Prolog says true instead of true. (i.e. no full-stop after true). Prolog does this when it believes it may be able to prove that the query is true in more than one way (& there are no variables in the query, that it can report bindings for).

Example: suppose we have the following facts and rule:

bad_dog(fido).

bad_dog(Dog) :-

bites(Dog, Person),

is_person(Person),

 is_dog(Dog).

bites(fido, postman).

is_person(postman).

is_dog(fido).

There are two ways to prove bad_dog(fido): (a) it's there as a fact; and (b) it can be proven using the bad_dog rule:

?- *bad_dog(fido).*
true *;*
true.

The missing full-stop prompts us to type ; if we want to check for another proof. The true. that follows means that a second proof *was* found. Alternatively, we can just press the "return" key if we are not interested in whether there is another proof.

Review questions

1. Describe the difference between procedural approach (procedural language) and declarative approach (declarative language) of programming? Discuss the merit and demerit of them with ideal/practical example. Describe Prolog as a declarative language.

2. Do you think that declarative languages have their own limitations?

3. Open Prolog and see the difference of prolog run time environment with other programming software's

4. Consider the following information and try to code using Prolog

   o An elephant is bigger than a horse.

   o A horse is bigger than a donkey.

   o A donkey is bigger than a monkey

5. Identify objects in your class room by your own and do the following

   o Tell us the description of the object

   o Attempt to represent your descriptions using prolog

6. Convert the following prolog statements into English statements

   o eats(bekele, orange).

   o likes(jhon, football).

   o likes(jhon, football, swimming, watching_movie).

   o not(likes(abebe, hardwork)).

7. Represent the following fact with prolog and save it with your own file name Load the above created file (file->consult->locate and open the file in the dialog box) and ask the following question to your program and evaluate why the system responds Yes/ True or No/False.

Fido is dog.

Rover is dog.

Henry is dog.

Felix is cat.

Michael is cat.

Jane is cat.

a) Is fido a dog?

b) Is jane a dog?

c) List down all dogs?

d) What other possible questions you can ask to your program?

8. Based on the knowledge base stated below, answer the following questions and trace how the solution is gained

% studies(X,Y):person X studies in course Y

studies(fred, 9020).

studies(jack, 9311).

studies(jill, 9314).

studies(jill, 9414).

studies(henry, 9414).

studies(henry, 9314).

% year(X, Y): person X is in year Y

year(fred, 1).

year(jack, 2).

year(jill, 2).

year(henry, 4).

a) How many students are involved in a course study?

b) how many courses are given in a study?

c) how many courses are taken by student Jill?

d) How many students take course 9414

9. Indicate whether the following are syntactically correct rules.

    a) a :- b, c, d:- e f.

    b) happy(X):- a , b.

    c) happy(X):- hasmoney(X) & has_friends(X).

    d) fun(fish):- blue(betty), bike(yamaha).

10. Consider the following fact and answer questions below

dog(fido).	cat(felix).
dog(rover).	cat(michael).
dog(henry).	cat(jane).

    a) Is fido an animal? Trace how the program prove if fido an animal or not.

    b) Write a rule that *rule* saying that anything (let us call it X) is an animal if it is a dog.

    c) Write a rule that *rule* saying that anything (let us call it X) is an animal if it is a dog or cat.

    d) Write a rule that *rule* saying that anything (let us call it X) is an animal if it is a dog and cat.

    e) Write a rule that *rule* saying that anything (let us call it X) is an animal if it is a dog and cat and it has four legs.

    f) What further facts can you include to your program to make this rule true.

11. Create a family tree program to include following rules –convert into prolog rules (4 pts)

    a) F is the father of P *if* he is a parent of P and is male

    b) M is the mother of P *if* she is a parent of P and is female

    c) X is a sibling of Y *if* they both have the same parent.

    d) Then add rules for grandparents, uncle, aunt, sister and brother.

12. Given the knowledge base below, study the queries underneath it.

likes(john,mary).

likes(john,trains).

likes(peter,fast_cars).

hobby(john,trainspotting).

hobby(tim,sailing).

hobby(helen,trainspotting).

hobby(simon,sailing).

    a) write a rule that says *two persons like each other if they have the same hobby*

    b) Indicate whether you think a particular query will succeed or fail by answer yes or no.

    ?- likes(john,trains).

    ?- likes(helen,john).

    ?- likes(tim,helen).

    ?- likes(john,helen).

Chapter Four

Predicates in prolog

At the end of this chapter, learners should be able to:

- Know and use various types of built-in functions in Prolog.

- Understand and use type checking & input/output predicates in prolog.

- Understand how to create user defined predicates

- Include and use user defined predicates into their programs

Predicates

Functions, in Prolog, are often called predicates. They are series of codes that perform a specific task. Like other programming languages, Prolog has **built-in functions** that perform defined purposes or allow users to define their own functions, **user defined functions**.

Built in predicates

Type checking predicates

The following list of built in predicates are used when checking the types of a given argument or terms. The predicates include:

atom/1: *Usage: atom(argument)*

Succeeds if argument is either an atom or a variable that has been previously instantiated to an atom. We can use this predicate to check whether the given argument is an atom or not.

Examples

?- atom(abc).
Yes
?- A = abc, atom(A).
A = abc ;
Yes
?- atom(male(abebe)).
No

compound/1: Usage: compound(*argument*)

Succeeds if argument is instantiated to a structured data object (predicate (compound term) or a list). We can use this predicate to check whether the given argument is a predicate, list or not.

Examples

?- compound(a(X)).
Yes
?- compound([a, B]).
Yes
?-compount(abebe).
No

float/1, integer/1, number/1: Usage: float(*argument*), integer(*argument*), number(*argument*).

float/1 will succeed if argument is a float number or a variable that has been previously instantiated to a float.

integer/1 will succeed if argument is an integer or a variable that has been previously instantiated to an integer.

number/1 will succeed if argument is a number (either integer or float) or a variable that has been previously instantiated to a number,

Examples

> ?- *float(12.23))*.
>
> Yes
>
> ?- *integer(5)*.
>
> Yes
>
> ?-*float(abebe)*.
>
> No
>
> ?-*integer(animal(dog))*.
>
> No
>
> ?-*number(3)*.
>
> Yes

var/1,nonvar/1: Usage: **var**(*argument*), nonvar(*argument*)

var/1 will succeed if argument is an uninstantiated variable. Note that if a variable has been previously instantiated (given a value), then var/1 will fail. We can use this predicate to check whether the given argument is a variable.

Examples

    ?- A = abc, var(A). % A has a value there fore prolog will answer no

        No

    ?- var(solomon).   % solomon is not a variable so prolog will answer no

        No

    ?-var(X).

        Yes

nonvar/1 will succeed if argument is *not* an uninstantiated variable. Note that if a variable has been previously instantiated, then nonvar/1 will succeed. We can use this predicate to check whether the given argument is not variable.

Examples

    ?- A = abc, nonvar(A).

        Yes

    ?- nonvar(solomon). % solomon is not a variable so prolog will answer yes

        Yes

    ?-nonvar(X).

        No

Input and output predicates

The following list of built in predicates are used for inputting and outputting terms in prolog.

write/1: Usage: write(*argument*)

Displays the argument in the bracket, to the current output stream (the system prompt). The argument must be a valid prolog term or a text enclosed in a single quotes.

Examples

   ?- *write(abc).*

  abc

   ?- *write('the day is very hot').*

The day is very hot

read/1: Usage: read(*variable*)

Requires the user to input a valid prolog term and unifies (assigns) the entered term

to the variable in the bracket.

Examples ?- *read(Abc).*   *% the term in the brace must be a variable.*

          |: 'the day is hot' *% it waits for the user to input a valid term*

          X = the day is hot *% X is assigned the entered term*

          ?- *read(animal(X)).*

              |: animal(dog).

              X = animal(dog)

nl/0: Usage: nl

prints a new line to the current output stream (the system prompt).

   ?- *write(a) , nl , write(b).*

put/1: Usage: put(*argument*)

Is used to output characters to the system prompt. The argument is an ASCII code

representing the character to be displayed and is a numeric values from $0 - 255$.

ASCII code of a, N and \ is 97, 78 and 92 respectively

Examples

   ?- *put(97).*
   a
   ?- put(78).
   N
   ?- put(92).
   \

get/1, get0/1: Usage: get(Variable), get0(Variable)

Is used to input characters from the system prompt. Requires the user to enter a single character and assigns the ASCII code of the inputted character to the variable.

Examples

   ?- *get(X).*
   |: a   % no full stop is necessary here.
   X = 97
   ?- *get0(M).*
   |: \   % no full stop is necessary here.
   X = 92

Some others useful predicates

True

The goal True/0 always succeeds.

   father(jim,fred).
   is in fact equivalent to :
   father=(jim,fred) :- true.

repeat

The goal repeat/0 is used to do a loop. The predicate in which it is used is repeated until every goal succeeds. Example :

```
test :- repeat,
        write('Please enter a number'),
        read(X),
        (X=:=42).
```

In this example the program will ask you to enter a number until you enter 42.

Call

This predicate is used to launch another predicat. For example call(p) will run p.

Example :

```
call(write((``Hello World!",nl))).
```

Note that we can't write call(write('Hello World'),nl). because the predicate call/2 is not avaible in every Prolog.

Setof

setof/3 can be usefull if you want to find all the solutions of a predicate. For example if we have this database :

```
knows(jim,fred).
knows(alf,bert).
```

If we want to find all the solutions of knows(X,Y). we can enter :

```
setof([X,Y],knows(X,Y),Z).
Z = [[jim,fred],[alf,bert]]
```

bagof

Bagof/3 is similar to setof/3. The difference is that bageof/3 leaves all repeated solutions while setof/3 removes them.

Note: Prolog has hundreds of built in predicates each with their own purpose. Find out them!

The is operator

- The right hand argument of is must be an arithmetic expression that can be evaluated right now (no unbound variables).
- This expression is evaluated and bound to the left hand argument.
- is is not a C-style assignment statement:
  - X is X + 1 won't work!
  - except via backtracking, variables can only be bound once, using is or any other way
- = does not cause evaluation of its arguments:

  > ?- $X = 2, Y = X + 1.$?- $X = 2, Y$ is $X + 1.$
  > X = 2   X = 2
  > Y = 2+1   Y = 3

- Use is if and only if you need to evaluate something:

  > *X is 1 BAD!   - nothing to evaluate*
  > *X = 1 GOOD!*

Order of goals with *is*

- Order of goals matters with is.

Variables on the RHS of is *must* be instantiated at the time the is goal is tried by Prolog. This is why the following example fails:

?- X is Y + 1, Y = 3.

ERROR: is/2: Arguments are not sufficiently instantiated

vs

?- Y = 3, X is Y + 1.

Y = 3,

X = 4.

is, = and =:=

- You can see the differences between these three Prolog constructs from the following example Prolog queries:

?- X =:= 3+2. ERROR: =:=/2: Arguments are not sufficiently instantiated	X is not currently bound, so can't be evaluated.
?- X = 3+2. X = 3+2.	= doesn't evaluate, so X is bound to 3+2.
?- X is 3+2. X = 5.	is *does* evaluate its right-hand side.
?- 4+1 is 3+2. false.	3+2 is evaluated to 5. 4+1 is not evaluated. So 4+1 is different from 5.
?- 4+1=3+2. false.	Neither side is evaluated by =. The two expressions are different.
?- 4+1 =:= 3+2. true.	Both sides are evaluated by =:=

= is used for matching, so a more appropriate use would be:

?- likes(mary, X) = likes(Y, pizza).

X = pizza,

Y = mary.

NB: Prolog has hundreds of built-in functions. You can open your Prolog software and practice all of these to better understand built-in predicate. Type "help." and enter in the prolog environment to continue practicing prolog built-in predicates and their usage

User Defined functions in PROLOG

We can also create our own functions in prolog and the functions are called user defined functions. You can work out your function by calling in the Prolog environment.

Example: a function that adds to numbers accepting from the user

add:- write('enter two numbers'),nl,
    read(X), read(Y),nl,
    Z= X+Y,
    write(Z).

so we can query as

    ?-add.

        // follow the prompt

Review question

1. Write a prolog program that displays "hello world".

2. Write a prolog program that prompts you for your name, then accepts you name and displays

   Hello <your name>
   Welcome to prolog"

3. Write a prolog program that identify a given string is

   a) a variable or a value

   b) a word or a number

   c) a compound or an atom

4. Write a prolog program that can do the following by creating your own functions

   a) list days of a week

   b) list months of a year

   c) performs arithmetic's of two numbers

Chapter Four

Structures in Prolog

At the end of this chapter, learners should be able to:

- Understand how to use complex data structures into their program

- Understand how to ask questions (query) items from structures

- Write and trace back the operation and execution of recursive structures

- Understand & identify built in functions to control the execution of recursive structures

Data Structures

Functional terms can be used to construct complex data structures. If we want to say that John owns the novel Tehanu, we can write: *owns(john, 'Tehanu')*. Often objects have a number of attributes: *owns(john, book('Tehanu', leguin))*. The author LeGuin has attributes too: *owns(john, book('Tehanu', author (leguin, ursula)))*. The arity of a term is the number of arguments it takes. All versions of owns have arity 2, but the detailed structure of the arguments changes.

For example, *gives(john, book, mary).* is a term with arity 3.

Asking Questions with Structures

How do we ask, "What books does John own that were written by someone called LeGuin"?

> ?- *owns(john, book(Title, author(leguin, GivenName)))*.
> Title = 'Tehanu'
> GivenName = ursula

What books does John own?

> ?- *owns(john, Book)*.
> Book = book('Tehanu', author(leguin, ursula))

What books does John own?

> ?- *owns(john, book(Title, Author))*.
> Title = 'Tehanu'
> Author = author(leguin, ursula)

Prolog performs a complex matching operation between the structures in the query and those in the clause head.

Example: Library Database

— A database of books in a library contains facts of the form

book(CatalogNo, Title, author(Family, Given)).

libmember(MemberNo, name(Family, Given), Address).

loan(CatalogNo, MemberNo, BorrowDate, DueDate).

— A member of the library may borrow a book.

- A "loan" records:

  - the catalogue number of the book

  - the number of the member

  - the date on which the book was borrowed

  - the due date

Example 2: Library Database

- Dates are stored as structures:

  date(Year, Month, Day).

- e.g. date(2012, 6, 16) represents 16 June 2012.

- which books has a member borrowed?

  borrowed(MemFamily, Title, CatalogNo) :-

  libmember(MemberNo, name(MemFamily, _), _),

  loan(CatalogNo, MemberNo, _, _),

  book(CatalogNo, Title, _).

- The underscore or "don't care" variables (_) are used because for the purpose of this query we don't care about the values in some parts of these structures.

Comparison in PROLOG

We would like to know which books are overdue; how do we compare dates?

later(Date1, Date2) if Date1 is after Date2:

later(date(Y, M, Day1), date(Y, M, Day2)) :-

```
            Day1 > Day2.
    later(date(Y, Month1, _), date(Y, Month2, _)) :-
            Month1 > Month2.
    later(date(Year1, _, _), date(Year2, _, _)) :-
            Year1 > Year2.
```

This rule has three clauses: in any given case, only one clause is appropriate. They are tried in the given order. This is how disjunction (**or**) is often achieved in Prolog. In effect, we are saying that the first date is later than the second date if Day1 > Day2 and the Y and M are the same, **or** if the Y is the same and Month1 > Month2, **or** if Year1 > Year2.

NB: if the year and month are the same, then the heads of all three rules match, and so, while the first rule is the appropriate one, all three will be tried in the course of backtracking. However, the condition "Month1 > Month2" in the second rule means that it will fail in this case, and similarly for the third rule.

In the code for later, again we are using the comparison operator ">". More complex arithmetic expressions can be arguments of comparison operators.

Example, X + Y >= Z * W * 2.

The available *numeric* comparison operators are:

Operator	Meaning	Syntax
>	greater than	Expression1 > Expression2
<	less than	Expression1 < Expression2
>=	greater than or equal to	Expression1 >= Expression2
=<	less than or equal to	Expression1 =< Expression2
=:=	equal to	Expression1 =:= Expression2
=\=	not equal to	Expression1 =\= Expression2

All these numerical comparison operators evaluate both their arguments. That is, they evaluate Expression1 and Expression2.

Recursive Programs

Binary Trees

In the library database example, some complex terms contained other terms, for example, book contained name. The following term also contains another term, this time one similar to itself:

    tree(tree(L1, jack, R1), fred, tree(L2, jill, R2))

The variables L1, L2, R1, and R2 should be bound to sub-trees (this will be clarified shortly).

A structure like this could be used to represent a "binary tree" that looks like:

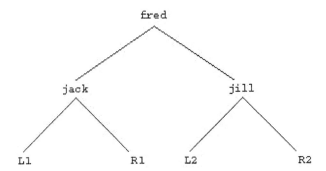

Binary because each "node" has two branches (our backtrack tree before had many branches at some nodes)

Recursive Structures

A term that contains another term that has the same principal functor (in this case tree) is said to be recursive. Biological trees have leaves. For us, a *leaf* is a node with two empty branches:

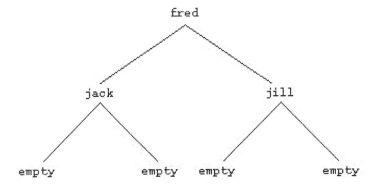

empty is an arbitrary symbol to represent the empty tree. In full, the tree above would be:

tree(tree(empty, jack, empty), fred, tree(empty, jill, empty)).

Usually, we wouldn't bother to draw the empty nodes:

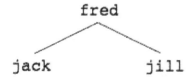

Another Tree Example

tree(tree(empty, 7, empty),

'+',

tree(tree(empty, 5, empty),

'-',

tree(empty, 3, empty))).

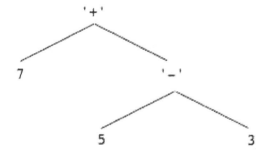

Recursive Programs for Recursive Structures

A binary tree is either empty or contains some data and a left and right subtree that are also binary trees. In Prolog we express this as:

```
is_tree(empty).            trivial branch
is_tree(tree(Left, Data, Right)) :-   recursive branch
    is_tree(Left),
    some_data(Data),
    is_tree(Right).
```

A non-empty tree is represented by a 3-arity term.

Any recursive predicate must have:

- (at least) one **recursive branch/rule** (or it isn't recursive :-)) and
- (at least) one non-recursive or **trivial branch** (to stop the recursion going on for ever).

The example at the heading "An Application of Lists", below, will show how the recursive branch and the trivial branch work together. However, you probably shouldn't try to look at it until we have studied lists.

Let us define (or measure) the size of tree (i.e. number of nodes):

```
tree_size(empty, 0).
tree_size(tree(L, _, R), Total_Size) :-
    tree_size(L, Left_Size),
    tree_size(R, Right_Size),
    Total_Size is
        Left_Size + Right_Size + 1.
```

Tree of size 5

The size of an empty tree is zero. The size of a non-empty tree is the size of the left sub-tree plus the size of the right sub-tree plus one for the current tree node. The data does not contribute to the total size of the tree. Recursive data structures need recursive programs. A recursive program is one that refers to itself, thus, tree_size contains goals that call for the tree_size of smaller tre

Example: The best way in Prolog to calculate a factorial is to do it recursively. Here is an example of how it can be done:

```
factoriel(0,1).
factoriel(X,Y) :-
            X1 is X - 1,
            factoriel(X1,Z),
            Y is Z*X,!.
?- factoriel(5,X).
X = 120
Yes/true
```

Controlling Execution

The Cut Operator (!)

Sometimes we need a way to prevent Prolog finding all solutions, i.e. a way to stop backtracking. The cut operator, written !, is a built-in goal that prevents backtracking. It turns Prolog from a nice declarative language into a hybrid monster. It use cuts sparingly and with a sense of having sinned.

Recall this example:

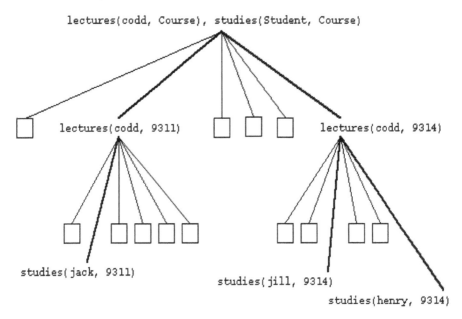

Cut Prunes the Search Tree

If the goal(s) to the right of the cut fail then the entire clause fails and the the goal that caused this clause to be invoked fails.

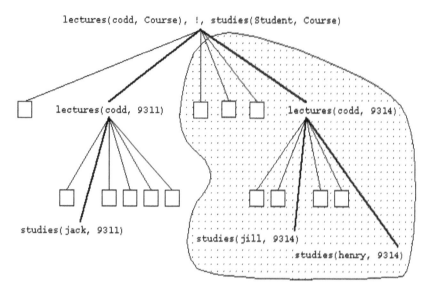

In particular, alternatives for Course are not explored. Another example: using the

facts03 database, try

> ?- *lectures(codd, X).*
> X = 9311 ;
> X = 9314.
> ?- *lectures(codd, X), ! .*
> X = 9311.

The cut in the second version of the query prevents Prolog from backtracking to

find the second solution. Using cuts in later to improve efficiency

Recall the code for later:

> later(date(Y, M, D1), date(Y, M, D2)) :- D1 > D2.
> later(date(Y, M1, _), date(Y, M2, _)) :- M1 > M2.
> later(date(Y1, _, _), date(Y2, _, _)) :- Y1 > Y2.

We note that if year and month are the same, all three rules are tried while backtracking. This could be prevented by adding cuts:

later(date(Y, M, D1), date(Y, M, D2)) :- D1 > D2, !.

later(date(Y, M1, _), date(Y, M2, _)) :- M1 > M2, !.

later(date(Y1, _, _), date(Y2, _, _)) :- Y1 > Y2.

This would increase efficiency by eliminating unnecessary backtracking, though it is doubtful if it would be worth bothering about, unless you actually have code that is running too slowly. In that case you should first do an analysis of where the time is being spent, before putting in cuts everywhere! In other cases, adding cuts of this sort to multi-rule procedures might be a useful (if lazy) way of ensuring that only one rule is used in a particular case. Unless it makes the code very clumsy, it is better to use and rely on "condition" goals in each rule (like M1 > M2 in the second rule for later) to specify the case in which it is appropriate. More examples of this are below.

Another cut example

max, without cut:

```
% max(A, B, C) binds C to the larger of A and B.
max(A, B, A) :- A > B.
max(A, B, B) :-A =< B.
max, with cut:
max(A, B, A) :- A > B, !.
max(A, B, B).
```

The first version has a negated test in the second rule (=< vs >). The second version substitutes a cut in the first rule for the negated test.

Another cut example

```
remove_dups, without cut:
remove_dups([], []).
remove_dups([First | Rest], NewRest) :-
   member(First, Rest),
   remove_dups(Rest, NewRest).
remove_dups([First | Rest], [First | NewRest]) :-
   not(member(First, Rest)),
remove_dups(Rest, NewRest).
remove_dups, with cut:
remove_dups([], []).
remove_dups([First | Rest], NewRest) :-
   member(First, Rest), !,
   remove_dups(Rest, NewRest).
remove_dups([First | Rest], [First | NewRest]) :-
remove_dups(Rest, NewRest).
```

The first version has a negated test in the third rule (not(member(First, Rest))). The second version substitutes a cut in the second rule for the negated test in the third rule.

Review Questions

1. The following are a prolog program that can show us the overdue and due date for a Library database. Improve the program to a full library database application for a simple Library automation Project.

   a prolog code for: Overdue Books

   > overdue(Today, Title, CatalogNo, MemFamily):
   >
   > given the date Today, produces the Title, CatalogNo,
   >
   > and MemFamily of all overdue books.
   >
   > overdue(Today, Title, CatalogNo, MemFamily) :-
   >
   > loan(CatalogNo, MemberNo, _, DueDate),
   >
   > later(Today, DueDate),
   >
   > book(CatalogNo, Title, _),
   >
   > libmember(MemberNo, name(MemFamily, _), _).

   a prolog code for Due Date of items - *a*ssume the loan period is one month:

   > due_date(date(Y, Month1, D),
   >
   >   date(Y, Month2, D)) :-
   >
   >   Month1 < 12,
   >
   >   Month2 is Month1 + 1.
   >
   > due_date(date(Year1, 12, D),
   >
   >   date(Year2, 1, D)) :-
   >
   >   Year2 is Year1 + 1.

69

2. Use recursive structures to develop a program using PROLOG for the following applications

   a) the sum of the first 100 natural numbers

   b) the sum of the first 100 odd natural numbers

   c) the sum of the first 100 even natural numbers

   d) the ASCII code for the 10 consecutive numbers

   e) the numeric representation for capital & small English Alphabets

Chapter Five

Lists and File in PROLOG

At the end of this chapter, learners should be able to:

- Define list and its operation in Prolog.

- Write code that can construct members of a list.

- Concatenate two or more lists into one program.

- Read and write contents from & into file

List

A list may be nil (i.e. empty) or it may be a term that has a **head** and a **tail**. The head may be any term or atom. The tail is another list. We could define lists as follows:

is_list(nil).

is_list(list(Head, Tail)) :- is_list(Tail).

A list of numbers [1, 2, 3] would look like:

list(1, list(2, list(3, nil)))

This notation is understandable but clumsy. Prolog doesn't actually recognise it, and in fact uses . instead of list and [] instead of nil. So Prolog would recognise .(1, .(2, .(3, []))) as a list of three numbers. This is briefer but still looks strange, and is

hard to work with. Since lists are used so often, Prolog in fact has a special
notation that encloses the list members in square brackets:

$$[1, 2, 3] = .(1, .(2, .(3, [])))$$
$$?- X = .(1, .(2, .(3, []))).$$
$$X = [1, 2, 3]$$

List Constructor |

Within the square brackets [ ], the symbol | acts as an operator to construct a list
from an item and another list.

$$?- X = [1 | [2, 3]].$$
$$X = [1, 2, 3].$$
$$?- Head = 1 , Tail = [2, 3], List = [Head | Tail].$$
$$List = [1, 2, 3].$$

Examples of Lists and Pattern Matching

?- [X, Y, Z] = [1, 2, 3].	Match the terms on either side of =
X = 1	
Y = 2	
Z = 3	
?- [X	Y] = [1, 2, 3].	| separates head from tail of list.
X = 1	So [First | Rest] is the usual way
Y = [2, 3]	of writing .(First, Rest) in Prolog
?- [X	Y] = [1].	The empty list is written as []
X = 1	Lists "end" in an empty list!
Y = []	Note that [1] is a list with one element.

The first several elements of the list can be selected before matching the tail:

> ?- *[X, Y | Z] = [fred, jim, jill, mary]*.
>
> X = fred   Must be at least two elements
>
> Y = jim   in the list on the right.
>
> Z = [jill, mary]

More Complex List Matching

> ?- *[X | Y] = [[a, f(e)], [n, m, [2]]]*.
>
> X = [a, f(e)]
>
> Y = [[n, m, [2]]]

Notice that Y is shown with an extra pair of brackets: Y is the tail of the entire list: [n, m, [2]] is the sole element of Y.

List Membership

A term is a member of a list if the term is the same as the head of the list, or the term is a member of the tail of the list.

In Prolog:

member(X, [X | _]).
             trivial branch:

             a rule with a head but no body

member(X, [_ | Y]) :-
             recursive branch
    member(X, Y).

The first rule has the same effect as: member(X, [Y|_]) :- X = Y. The form member(X, [X|_]). is preferred, as it avoids the extra calculation. member is actually predefined in Prolog. It is a built-in predicate.

= in goals

Earlier, we said:

    X = 1   GOOD!

Actually, goals with = in them are mostly avoidable and *should* be avoided. Beginnner Prolog programmers are tempted to use = frequently, to tie together variables that they now realise should be the same:

    % length(List, LengthOfList)

    % binds LengthOfList to the number of elements in List.

    length([OnlyMember], Length) :-

      Length = 1.

    length([First | Rest], Length) :-

      length(Rest, LengthOfRest),

      Length is LengthOfRest + 1.

This works, but involves an unnecessary unification. It is better for the base case to be

    length([OnlyMember], 1).

In effect, we take the original version of the base case, and replace Length, in the head of the rule, with the thing that Length is = to. Programmers who fail to do this are usually still thinking procedurally.

Concatenating Two Lists

Suppose we want to take two lists, like [1, 3] and [5, 2] and concatenate them to make [1, 3, 5, 2]

The header comment is:

    % concat(List1, List2, Concat_List1_List2)

    % Concat_List1_List2 is the concatenation of List1 & List2

There are two rules: First, the trivial branch:

    concat([], List2, List2).

Next, the recursive branch:

    concat([Item | Tail1], List2, [Item | Concat_Tail1_List2]) :-

    concat(Tail1, List2, Concat_Tail1_List2).

For example, consider

    ?- concat([1], [2], [1, 2]).

By the recursive branch:

    concat([1 | []], [2], [1 | [2]]) :-

    concat([], [2], [2]).

and concat([], [2], [2]) holds because of the trivial branch.

The entire program is:

```
% concat(List1, List2, Concat_List1_List2):
%   Concat_List1_List2 is the concatenation of List1 & List2
concat([], List2, List2).
concat([Item | Tail1], List2, [Item | Concat_Tail1_List2]) :-
concat(Tail1, List2, Concat_Tail1_List2).
```

Example: An Application of Lists - find the total cost of a list of items:

Cost data:

```
cost(cornflakes, 230).
cost(cocacola, 210).
cost(chocolate, 250).
cost(crisps, 190).
```

Rules:

```
total_cost([], 0).              % trivial branch
total_cost([Item|Rest], Cost) :-  % recursive branch
        cost(Item, ItemCost),
        total_cost(Rest, CostOfRest),
        cost is ItemCost + CostOfRest.
```

Sample query:

```
?- total_cost([cornflakes, crisps], X).
```

X = 420

Tracing total_cost

?- *trace.*

true.

[trace] ?- *total_cost([cornflakes, crisps], X).*

  Call: (7) total_cost([cornflakes, crisps], _G290) ? creep

  Call: (8) cost(cornflakes, _L207) ? creep

  Exit: (8) cost(cornflakes, 230) ? creep

  Call: (8) total_cost([crisps], _L208) ? creep

  Call: (9) cost(crisps, _L228) ? creep

  Exit: (9) cost(crisps, 190) ? creep

  Call: (9) total_cost([], _L229) ? creep

  Exit: (9) total_cost([], 0) ? creep

^ Call: (9) _L208 is 190+0 ? creep

^ Exit: (9) 190 is 190+0 ? creep

  Exit: (8) total_cost([crisps], 190) ? creep

^ Call: (8) _G290 is 230+190 ? creep

^ Exit: (8) 420 is 230+190 ? creep

  Exit: (7) total_cost([cornflakes, crisps], 420) ? creep

  X = 420

  [debug] ?- *notrace.*

Another list-processing procedure

The next procedure removes duplicates from a list. It has *three rules*. This is an example of a common list-processing *template*.

Algorithm:

I.   If the list is empty, there's nothing to do.

II.   If the first item of the list is a member of the rest of the list, then discard it, and remove duplicates from the rest of the list.

III. Otherwise, keep the first item, and again, remove any duplicates from the rest of the list.

% remove_dups(+List, -NewList):

% New List isbound to List, but with duplicate items removed.

remove_dups([], []).

remove_dups([First | Rest], NewRest) :-

   member(First, Rest),

   remove_dups(Rest, NewRest).

remove_dups([First | Rest], [First | NewRest]) :-

   not(member(First, Rest)),

   remove_dups(Rest, NewRest).

?- remove_dups([1,2,3,1,3,4], X).

X = [2, 1, 3, 4];

false.

Note the use of not to negate a condition.

File in PROLOG

Writing to Files

Many applications require that output be written to a file rather than to the screen. In this section we will explain how to do this in Prolog.

In order to write to a file we have to create one (or open an existing one) and associate a stream with it. You can think of streams as connections to files. In Prolog, streams are blessed with names in a rather user-unfriendly format, such as '\$stream'(183368) . Luckily, you never have to bother about the exact names of streams — although Prolog assigns these names internally, you can use Prolog's unification to match the name to a variable and make use of the variable rather than the name of the stream itself.

The inbuilt predicate open/3 opens a file and connects it to a stream.

open(+*FileName*,+*Mode*,-*Stream*).

The first argument of open is the name of the file, and in the last argument, Prolog returns the name that it assigns to the stream. *Mode* is one of read, write, append. read means that the file is opened for reading, and write and append both open the file for writing. In both cases, the file is created, if it doesn't exist, yet. If it does exist, however, write will cause the file to be overwritten, while append appends everything at the end of the file.

When you are finished with the file, you should close it again. That is done with the following predicate, where *Stream* is the name of a Stream as assigned by Prolog.

    close(*Stream*).

So, programs that are writing to or reading from files will typically have the following structure:

    open(myfile,write,Stream),
    ...
      do something
        ...
    close(Stream),

Say you want to print the string 'Hogwarts' to the file hogwarts.txt . This is done as follows:

    ...
    open('hogwarts.txt',write,Stream),
    write(Stream,'Hogwarts'), nl(Stream),
    close(Stream),
    ...

What's happening here? Well, first the built-in predicate open/3 is used to create the file hogwarts.txt. The second argument of open/3 indicates that we want to open a new file (overwriting any existing file with the same name). The third argument of open/3 returns the name of the stream. Secondly, we write 'Hogwarts' on the stream and issue a newline command as well. After this we are ready, and close the stream, using the built-in close/1.

And that's more or less all there is to it. As promised, we were not interested in the name of the stream — we used the variable Stream to pass it around. Also note that the write/2 predicate we used here is basically a more general form of the write/1 predicates.

What if you don't want to overwrite an existing file but append to an existing one? This is done by choosing a different mode when opening the file: instead of write, use append as value for the second argument of open/3. If a file of the given name doesn't exist, it will be created.

Reading from Files

In this section we show how to read from files. Reading information from files is straightforward in Prolog — or at least, it is if this information is given in the form of Prolog terms followed by full stops.

Finally, there is a two-place predicate for reading in terms from a stream. read always looks for the next term on the stream and reads it in.

> read(+*Stream*,+*Term*)

Consider the file houses.txt :

> gryffindor.
> hufflepuff.
> ravenclaw.
> slytherin.

Here is a Prolog program that opens this file, reads the information from it, and displays it on the screen:

```
main:-
    open('houses.txt',read,Str),
    read(Str,House1),
    read(Str,House2),
    read(Str,House3),
    read(Str,House4),
    close(Str),
    write([House1,House2,House3,House4]), nl.
```

This opens a file in reading mode, then reads four Prolog terms using the built-in predicate read/2 , closes the stream, and prints the information as a list.

All very straightforward. Nonetheless, the read/2 predicate needs to be handled with care. First of all, it only is able to handle Prolog terms (we'll say more about this problem shortly). And secondly, it will cause a run-time error if we use it to read from a stream when there is nothing to read. Is there an elegant way to overcome this second problem?

There is. The built-in predicate at_end_of_stream/1 checks whether the end of a stream has been reached, and can be used as a safety-net. For a stream X , at_end_of_stream(X) will evaluate to true when the end of the stream X is reached (in other words, when all terms in the corresponding file have been read).

The following code is a modified version of our earlier reading-in program, which shows how at_end_of_stream/1 can be incorporated:

```
main:-

        open('houses.txt',read,Str),
        read_houses(Str,Houses),
        close(Str),
         write(Houses), nl.


read_houses(Stream,[]):-
    at_end_of_stream(Stream).


read_houses(Stream,[X|L]):-
    \+ at_end_of_stream(Stream),
    read(Stream,X),
    read_houses(Stream,L).
```

Now for the nastier problem. Recall that read/2 only reads in Prolog terms. If you want to read in arbitrary input, things become rather unpleasant, as Prolog forces you to read information on the level of characters. The predicate that you need in this case is get_code/2 which reads the next available character from a stream. Characters are represented in Prolog by their integer codes. For example, get_code/2 will return 97 if the next character on the stream is an a.

Usually we are not interested in these integer codes, but in the characters — or rather, in the atoms that are made up of lists of these characters. How do we get our hands on these (lists of) characters? One way is to use the built-in predicate atom_codes/2 to convert a list of integers into the corresponding atom. We'll use this technique in the following example, a predicate that reads in a word from a stream.

```
readWord(InStream,W):-
    get_code(InStream,Char),
    checkCharAndReadRest(Char,Chars,InStream),
    atom_codes(W,Chars).
  checkCharAndReadRest(10,[],_):- !.
checkCharAndReadRest(32,[],_):- !.
checkCharAndReadRest(-1,[],_):- !.
checkCharAndReadRest(end_of_file,[],_):- !.
checkCharAndReadRest(Char,[Char|Chars],InStream):-
    get_code(InStream,NextChar),
    checkCharAndReadRest(NextChar,Chars,InStream).
```

How does this work? It reads in a character and then checks whether this character is a blank (integer code 32), a new line (10) or the end of the stream (− 1). In any of these cases a complete word has been read, otherwise the next character is read

Review Questions

1. How simple are file operation in Prolog?

2. Write code that creates hogwart.houses , a file that that looks like this:

       gryffindor
hufflepuff   ravenclaw
     slytherin

You can use the built-in predicates open/3 , close/1 , tab/2 , nl/1 , and write/2 .

3. Write a Prolog program that reads in a plain text file word by word, and asserts all read words and their frequency into the Prolog database. You may use the predicate readWord/2 to read in words. Use a dynamic predicate word/2 to store the words, where the first argument is a word, and the second argument is the frequency of that word.

4. Here is a piece of code , what will look like the output of the code.

?- open(hogwarts,write,OS),

  tab(OS,7),write(OS,gryffindor),nl(OS),

  write(OS,hufflepuff),tab(OS,5),write(OS,ravenclaw),nl(OS),

  tab(OS,7),write(OS,slytherin),

  close(OS).

References

[1] Davis, Randall, and Douglas B. Lenat. Expert Systems in Artificial
       Intelligence: Case   Studies. McGraw-Hill, Inc., 1982

[2]   Floyd, Robert W. "The paradigms of programming."
       Communications of the ACM 22.8 (1979): 455-460.

[3]   Nowak, Agnieszka, and Wykład IVa. "Prolog-Programming In Logic." :

[4]   Bratko, Ivan. Prolog programming for artificial intelligence. Pearson
       education, 2001.

[5]   Barr, A. and Feigenbaum, E.A. "The Handbook of Artificial Intelligence".
       New York: Addison-Wesley, 1989.

[6]   Pearson Education. "Chapter 18 - Knowledge Acquisition, Representation,
       and Reasoning", URL:
       http://wps.prenhall.com/ media/objects/Turban_Online_Chapter_W18.pdf

[7]   Wielemaker, Jan, S. Ss, and I. Ii. "SWI-Prolog 2.7-Reference Manual."
        URL: http://citeseerx.ist.psu.edu/viewdoc/summar, [April 2014].

[8] K. P. Tripathi. "A Review on Knowledge-based Expert System:
       Concept and Architecture." IJCA Special Issue on Artificial Intelligence Techniques
       - Novel Approaches & Practical   Applications, pp. 21-25, 2011.

[9]   Week, Business. "Artificial intelligence: the second computer age begins".
       Industrial edition,   No. 2729, pp.66-77, March 8, 1982.

[10] J.R.Fisher." Prolog Tutorial -- Introduction", URL: https://www.cpp.edu

www.ingramcontent.com/pod-product-compliance
Lightning Source LLC
LaVergne TN
LVHW042341060326
832902LV00006B/314